LIBER SIN NOMINE

(a book without name)

James Cowan

Balgo Hills
Publishing

Copyright © 2020 James Cowan

All rights reserved.

The author has asserted his right to be identified as the author of this work in accordance with the Copyright, Design and Patents Act 1988.

ISBN-13: 978-1-913816-08-7

Written by James Cowan in 2018

First published in this edition: 2020

Cover & Book Design: Amedée & Benjamin

SUMMA

Introduction by Solomon James	1
Plates	10
Exordium	13
Liber sin nomine	21
Post Verba	49

INTRODUCTION

Liber sin Nomine, or 'a book without name,' was James Cowan's final testament to this world. James Cowan made his passing from this life on 6th October 2018. The book was written in the final months leading up to October 2018.

This short book is itself a form of passage. It is a passage from the ancient heart of a deep, sacred human lineage, imbued with history - a tradition of the spirit - and into the modern heart of the dying moments of the author. Like much of James' work, it is a motif of establishing a thread to connect (or re-connect) to the living spirit that permeates the human life, and to make it relevant for the present time. James stated this clearly within the text. Even within his final moments, he was lucid on what his task was, and had always been: 'My task has always been to revive the concept of numen for a modern audience, to alert readers to a state of reverence present in all things.' James sought to revive the concept of numen for a modern audience. As he noted, the word '*numen*' suggests spirit, energy, and the sacred – and more. Almost within the same breath, James also declared that 'words and wandering share a unique symbiosis.' This is perhaps a window upon how we may consider the life and work of a unique individual. Through his endless wandering – both within the physical world as well as the metaphysical – he sought to find those words that could establish a communion, a communication, between the eternal sacred spirit and the forever changing heart of humankind.

Liber sin Nomine begins with an Exordium, or Introduction, where James relates his 2017 visit to the monastery of St. Gall by the shores of Lake Constance, Switzerland. The library of St. Gall is one of the oldest monastic libraries in the world and is recognized also as one of the richest medieval libraries with one of the most comprehensive collections of early medieval books in the German-speaking part of Europe. Yet James went for one book only: the *Evangelium longum* - a 'gem-encrusted tome made from silver and ivory, written in Latin, of St John's Gospel.' The book was fashioned by a monk known as Tuotilo who, it is said, created the book as a gift for Charlemagne. This book, as

James says, is 'a seamless expression of the sacred.' Viewing this book for the first time, and leafing through its pages with his gloved hands, was a revelatory experience for the septuagenarian James Cowan – 'I left the museum that day, conscious that I had been utterly transported.' The memory stayed with him and became the inspiration for this book that you now hold in your hands: 'This lead me to consider whether it might be possible, like Tuotilo and Sintram before me, to construct an entirely imaginary evangelium out of the tag-ends of my own thoughts.'

Yet James had no name for such a book – 'The question I next asked myself was: what should I call it?' And so, the book became the *Liber sin Nomine* (a book without name). It was James' original intention to create a type of spirit-full collection, or sacred 'tag-ends of my own thoughts.' In his final days he spoke of the book as an ongoing flow of thoughts and aphorisms. He often referred to it as 'my Aphorism book.' Yet it was more than a humble collection of 'tag-ends.' The book became James' own meditation on death and dying, and the relationship between a sacred life and the passing of that life.

Within the book there are various places where James Cowan is acutely aware of the nature of his dying body – also, the rebellious behaviour of his body. He states that, 'Let there be no mistake: my body has chosen to leave me! I did not give it permission to depart, at least not yet.' Here are the words of a heart and mind, an active and alert consciousness, coming to terms with a disintegrating, and dissenting, body: 'My body, now, is in violent disagreement with me. It simply refuses to concur with my pre-disposition towards health.'

The book without name is a reflection on the act of dying. It gives validation to a process of a physical slipping away with dignity and awareness. As a person who spent his life seeking to unravel the sacredness and mystery of life, James was now the participant in his own sacred passing, and witnessing first-hand the departure from a world he so lovingly, and desperately, sought to embrace: 'This is the nature of departure: to find the right words. No more metaphors, no more heartfelt sentences. Just the smooth transition into finitude.' James was aware he was now on the final stretch into a physical finitude. He was aware enough, and conscious, to give his consent to this final ride: 'I consent to death. It has made its demands, and I can no longer resist them.' This was also an opportunity (if we may be allowed to call it that) for a person to contemplate what the process of passing brings, and to become fully realized to the experience. In a sense, James was documenting his initiation into death: 'We have forgotten how to contemplate death *in* ourselves. Obviously it is there, a chrysalis in its cocoon. Our task is to unwind that golden thread and allow it to emerge, in its most precursal form, in order to become a fluttering moth. In that way we realise our own death rather than simply submitting to it.'

For James, the writing of the book was a tool that allowed him to 'realise' his death consciously rather than through an unconscious submission. He admitted that he had not 'interrogated' his illness – 'So far, I haven't interrogated my illness, at least not in so many words.' This was partly because he did not wish to become overly familiarized with it, for it is the familiar things that often slip unnoticed under our awareness. James wished to remain fully aware, and this is also perhaps why he refused to be tempted into giving the book a final naming: 'Most things, once they are named, enter a state of the familiar. I refuse to allow my condition to become so. I want to test its durability by leaving it unnamed.' And in this refusal to enter into a state of unconscious familiarity, or a drowsy submission, James was forced to face directly the oncoming arrival of his departure: 'I now know what death smells like. Of decay and deliquescence, the rapid disambiguation of being. It is in my nostrils now, a subtle stench that refuses to go away.'

Despite the severity of the situation, James, as the ever-curious seeker, was not without a sense of divine humour: 'If God give us strength to survive, then we suffer gravely when he goes on holidays.'

The act of facing oneself may also be seen as coming to terms with the 'Other.' It is an act of reconciliation; and for James, it perhaps represented the final act of his reconciliation. In one fine swoop, James elegantly brought closure to this through the recognition and acknowledgement that the Other was finally himself: 'This is the Other who is about to become myself. *He is me.*' This immaculate closure also seemed to bring into the fold his sense of destiny, as if the *amor fati* – or, love of one's fate – was finally coming home to rest: 'Frequently in my life have I encountered my Other as a positive influence, one governed by *amor fati*, my destiny.' In creating this closure, James also paid recognition to the presence of pain within life – a pain that was both individual and collective, as if each person had to endure some suffering as part of the collective healing. In one sense, individual pain blocks a person from their innate being: 'Pain is so immersive that it isolates the sufferer from being. One is forced to live in a kind of leprosarium of the mind.' And then there is the observer upon the world, who sees a form of 'noble suffering' as an act of redemption: 'At cafe tables and in bus terminals I have encountered the greatness and suffering of humanity.' In the Redeemer, the Christos of divine intervention, there is always a path to illumination - 'Grasp the light as if it were a nettle. Do not fear it.'

Within this nameless book, James also managed to place himself, in a more subtle sense, within a historic lineage of *sanguis*, or blood-relation of the spirit. This is a recognition that a 'loving knowledge,' or love through knowledge, is an act of transference that proceeds through the spirit-blood rather than through the physical blood bonds of heredity. James wrote that - 'Philosophers and emperors adopted young men as their heirs in thought and potential power. Parmenides adopted Zeno as his, Socrates that of Plato, and Emperor Augustus adopted Marcus Aurelius to succeed him.' Here was a form of bonding that strongly appealed to the sacrosanct part of his nature. Throughout his life, he had always maintained a 'spirit-blood' close circle of friends with whom he brought into a 'loving association' – often through a fellowship with the word and the spirit – that were distinct from his everyday circle of friends and acquaintances. James powerfully expressed this when he wrote - 'Men are drawn into loving association so that they might give a transfusion to one another.' [Men] here we can also take to represent the human being. This is an acknowledgement that there is a unique form of love – also, man-love – that is not sexual in nature but rather is the loving-knowledge transference that bonds people together through the spirit. And this, I would offer, is at the core of the life of James Cowan.

Here was a human being who sought for a sacred communion – a loving-knowledge transference or *transubstantiation* – between fellow souls.

Liber sin Nomine was to be an ongoing book. It only finished when it did because James himself finished. The author died and the book stopped with him. The words were flowing as an indication of his spirit, and both stopped flowing in physical form together. This is the reason why the book is the length it is. It is both a living as well as a dying testament. It is also the legacy of James Cowan and his lifetime search for the right words – or perhaps, for the Word itself. This may be one reason why James considered the aphorism as an appropriate form to express meaning: 'The aphorism is one way to revive words as a repository of meaning. It deepens it and complexifies the etymology of thought.' Also - 'The aphorism is like a scalpel; it cuts away dead flesh and helps to cleanse the wound of conventional expression. It becomes a mental abrasion that prepares the mind for new understanding, for an extension of consciousness.' James was forever attempting to 'cut away dead flesh' in order to get at the essentiality of words and their meaning. And this was perhaps his route to self-revelation.

For James Cowan, there was a direct relationship in the word as revelation. The word, and the careful sculpturing of the word, was itself an act of revelation. This was, in part, what drew him to the orthodoxy faith and especially to its manuscripts and illumined writings. James, we may say, was seeking the illumination of his self – or rather, *a revelation of himself* – through the word. It was the path to the miraculous, for to capture the miraculous is the responsibility and power – the duty – of the written word: 'Rather, the strange effervescence of a mind caught between two worlds – that of impending death and the unquenched vitality of an intellect on fire. This is what I wished to capture in my CODEX MIRACULUM.' In the final stroke, the book of 'no name' has the author's personal name – it was James Cowan's *Codex Miraculum* – his miraculous book or scroll. In other words, his very own 'word as revelation'. In fact, it was his final words; and in that, his final revelation to himself.

In the beginning was the Word…

Solomon James
November 2020

Evangelium Longum c.900 by Tuotilo

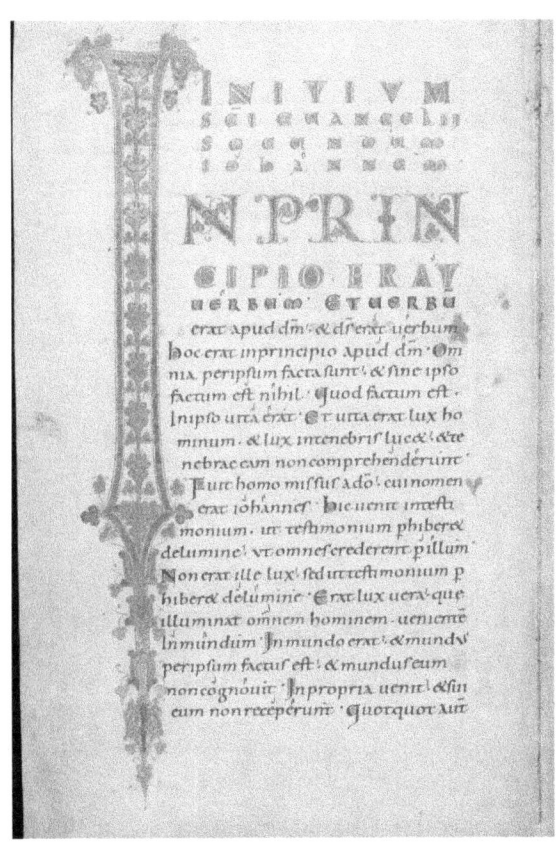

Title page of the Evangelium Longum by Sintram, John 1-14

EXORDIUM

    We are unfamiliar with the man known as Tuotilo other than that he was a monk residing in the monastery of St. Gall in the late ninth-century. What we do know about him, however, is that he was a master craftsman in silver and gold who fashioned many holy figures for churches and prominent benefactors throughout Northern Europe. His other talents are also instructive, in that he claimed to be a poet and a composer of church music. Broad-shouldered and rather massive as a man, a fine speaker such was it said of him, he nonetheless combined the delicacy of a craftsman with the delight in rendering his thoughts on parchment and vellum. The work that he is most famous for is a finely-crafted book known as the *Evangelium longum*, a gem-encrusted tome made from silver and ivory, written in Latin, of St John's Gospel. It is said that Tuotilo fashioned the book as a gift for Charlemagne.

The *Evangelium* is currently stored under lock and key in the library of St Gall by the shores of Lake Constance. I first set eyes on the book on a visit to the monastery in 2017. I was struck by its beauty and the remarkable illuminations that graced its pages. Here was a tome that glowed. It reminded me of the *Book of Kells*, of the patient work of Irish monks in their scriptoriums, and of their historic link to the monastery of St Gall. Celtic knots abounded on every introductory page throughout the work, much like butterflies fluttering above a field. I began to wonder whether such whorls and curvatures were designed to lure me into an unearthly construct. The inner world of a medieval spiritual, I finally decided, was as resplendent as the variegated colours found in a peacock's feathers.

Which lead me to ponder why such rare artifacts were fashioned in the first place. The idea that silver filigree and precious stones might be used to encase a book struck me as an unusual gesture whose motive was hard to fathom. Neither Greek nor Roman scribes made their scrolls into such objects of beauty. For them, a book was entirely utilitarian. The fashion for creating such elaborate tomes was very much a medieval and Christian practice, it seems. I decided then that there must be a subliminal link between rare gemstones, ivory, and precious metals that affirmed the dignity of words in themselves. They needed to be made into objects of beauty at the behest of pen and ink in order to satisfy our taste for the wholly other.

It is no accident, therefore, that our word 'wordsmith' is so closely aligned to that of 'silversmith' or indeed 'blacksmith'. Each endeavor suggests a careful manipulation of often intractable material not normally associated with well-executed and elegant formulations. The word 'decoration' also comes to mind. Words, when they are brought together in a text, become as keenly fashioned as any sword, broach, or reliquary. They produce awe, and thus require a master wordsmith to bless them with his craft.

Clearly Tuotilo understood such a relationship between metal, gemstones, and words. He worked alongside another monk, the scribe Sintram, who allowed his nibs to fashion their artifice with extraordinary medieval finesse. A specialist in illuminations, majuscule and uncial scripts, as well as their dramatic effects on the page, Tuotilo combined all these in his realization of a medieval masterpiece. Because of these two monks, the *Evangelium* transcends its properties as a book to become an object of distinct polyvalence and beauty. The good monks managed to create a book that was entirely comparable to its contents. St John, Tuotilo, and Sintram found themselves in league: inspiration, pen, metal files and mallets, together these made it possible for them to fashion the *Evangelium longum* into a seamless expression of the sacred.

    I left the museum that day, conscious that I had been utterly transported. The book I had so lovingly perused and hesitantly touched with my gloved hands, indeed marveled at, was now firmly lodged in my memory. Charlemagne may have opened it to read each evening as an act of devotion before he retired, but it was I who had now come into the possession of a different kind of text. My *Evangelium*, so to speak, had reached beyond its original encasement in silver and ivory to realize itself as an object of my imagination. In its own way it, too, had been transported.

This lead me to consider whether it might be possible, like Tuotilo and Sintram before me, to construct an entirely imaginary evangelium out of the tag-ends of my own thoughts. Of course, these monks were a silversmith and scribe who relied on practical applications to augment their purpose, whereas I would have to rely on another order of construction. My task, if I were to attempt it at all, would be to fabricate what the ancient Greeks called a "work of wonder" (*telesmi*) in order to fashion my own book into the depiction of some rare and refined pedigree. It would have to be a book that could only be rendered real by the imagination itself.

The question I next asked myself was: what should I call it? A Periplus, perhaps? Was my text to be the record of a voyage along the coastline of an entirely otherworldly continent, an Africa occidens of the mind? I then asked myself: should the words 'other' and 'world' be separated from one another in the quest for this name? The Real, after all, finds its origin in the idea of sanctum, a sanctuary, that place where invisible deities repose in order to keep cool during the heat of the day. Therefore, I decided, my text needed to imply something set apart, a 'sanctome' if you like, a book of rare and impecunious eloquence.

Yet the name of such a book escaped me, as much as I might have wished otherwise. I had not been able to extract its unique form from other extrapolations such as tablet, polytych, stele, cartulary, missal or even compendium. This imaginary book of mine thus awaits its final designation. Perhaps it will emerge as I write, who knows? Since it is a book that contains fire, light, and air, it needs to enact its own title from these febrile and distinctly luminous attributes. I can only hope that its name, its mysterious nomenclature still buried somewhere in the library of my mind, might arise, slowly, only when words themselves become filiations.

Here, therefore, are the contents of a book without name, the peregrinations of a mind that wishes to sail beyond Cape Bojador off the coast of Africa, a region that one poet informs us needs to be traversed if we are to pass beyond pain. This land, I suspect, is one that Tuotilo and Sintram understood better than most. For the challenge of creating a memorable book lies in acknowledging how transient language can be when detached from the fear of the ordinary. Books such as the *Evangelium longum*, like mine hopefully, must bear their thoughts with the same imperviousness to change as those gemstones and ivory reliefs implanted in its covers.

A BOOK WITHOUT NAME

Become a Stranger to yourself, I heard a voice whisper. Your solitude is as integral to life as the air we breathe. If a person seeks solace in the collective, he is already on the road to ruin. When words unite with meaning, then does a Solitary perceive his destiny. He becomes a mouthpiece for the veritable nature of truth extracted from what is essential in himself.

I have heard it said that men like the philosopher Parmenides and St Francis of Assisi were as strangers to themselves. They preferred to climb the rocky crags of certainty than to wander the flatlands of doubt. To them, solitude was a cool breeze that puckered their cheeks: a breath, a spirit leading them onwards, away from the ordinariness of speech.

The word 'cerebrum' and 'cherubim' sound almost the same. One intimates thought, the other the presence of an Angel. Can we not join these words together? Then we will have angelic thought, the divine attribute of reminiscence that hints at the eternal. How easy it would be then to smother disappointment under those cossetting wings that conceal the Stigmata of the Five Wounds – wounds that are none other than the revelations of the Angel. Such, too, is the cerebrum: a suscitation of wings, the joy of pure thought enacting the inconceivable.

They say that the moon is made up of lifeless matter, a dead thing suspended in space. And yet, does it not cling to the earth as an infant to its mother's breast? On certain evening it visits us as a golden orb, profoundly ornamental in the night sky, its nurturing delight a reflection of the sun's rays. No blue sky here, no clutter masquerading as 'atmosphere', just the inordinate glow of a moon whose father is the sun. Its existence, as such, transforms matter into the warmth of life itself.

Look upon all that you see and feel as if it were for the last time, this is what death urges me to do. Such an injunction I endure rather than accept. I am an acolyte in this respect, listening to my mentor who is a Stranger like myself. Ours is a collaborative effort: we are yearning to *give up* rather than to fight. The body, after all, has its own reasons for taking that lonely road. No one knows what lies ahead. A mountain range or an abyss, they are but inversions of one another.

Prayer is a strange discipline, it require a repetitive nature. Those who master it find themselves embarking on a voyage beyond words. No map yet devised acknowledges that last port-of-call. Portolan and compass, wind-rose and chart, they are but mental tools for navigation. Prayer, however, is a vast ocean not at all immune to the perturbations of the weather. When a storm approaches, consolation comes in the form of a stillness of mind. The ancients called this *apatheia*, the final renunciation of self.

The heart is a fragile craft. It awaits tide-turn before sailing forth. Who captains such a ship, I ask? Not the musculature of ventricle or auricle, those lifelong pump-actions of the body. No, the heart is diaphanous, transparent, a sure method for invigorating life. *This* is what presides over the call of coxswain and sailor reefing in sails. My heart has no figurehead at its bow. Rather, it points into the wind, its slender sprit participating in some figurative engagement with the unknown.

Welcome to this garden of delight, where tears are as nourishing as humus. Let them fall where they will. When a hermit surrenders to their caress, he knows they help him resist the alluring call of the desert. Tears, they say, are the salt of the earth. They pretend to be fluid, but really they are as solid as humility when cast up like flotsam on a beach. Only clowns can wear them as makeup; the rest of us must bear them as the importunity of grief.

Love, yes, I contend with it, this overarching largesse that speaks of contradiction and contentment. Who am I to denounce its opportunism in the wake of desire or yearning? All I know is that there are degrees of love, just as there are many fields of energy concealed in a magnet. Mine are concealed in the power of words. They energise my life, give it power to transform, act as quivering patterns capable of depicting the worthiness of love for me either to accept or reject.

I am fascinated by mandalas. Not those in Tibetan sand paintings, but the ones that crown the heads of saints. After all, they are halos that depict the luminous presence of everyone who has risen above the constraints of his ordinary nature. This is no mean feat. When a saint kneels before an image of his Redeemer, an act of obeisance vying with the pain in his arthritic knees, it is his halo that assures him of the prospect of receiving benediction and release.

I must begin this journey. My bag is packed. In memory I hear the sound of a semantron in a monastery courtyard, the dull thud of mallet against wood. This is my call to depart. It summons me to the cleansing darkness of dawn outside a Kathlikon after an all-night vigil inside. Candles glow above the iconostasis in my thoughts. I see holy figures emerge from the shadows. They, too, are urging me to set out. Where to, I ask? It is a question only incense harbour, sandalwood aglow and bells tinkling, the same solemn sound a bell-buoy tolls in a fog, signalling shallows, a sand bank.

The choice is stark. Either to fight to stay alive, with no surety of success. Or, to surrender to those beckoning gestures of the Queen of the Night, her tenebrous gaze more gentle than I am prepared to accept. Seductive? No, not really. But regal, one must admit. She handles darkness with the same consummate ease as a magician on-stage, waving his black cape to confuse his audience.

Let there be no mistake: my body has chosen to leave me! I did not give it permission to depart, at least not yet. Though it feels like a worn raffia mat under a rice barn, frayed and dishevelled, it offers some comfort, a sense of order and purpose. I sense, too, that it wishes to dispense with the newness of its past, which is no more if the truth be known, than a façade. Like an ascetic engaged in a long fast, this body of mine wishes to embrace slenderness, failing muscles and weakness, in its bid to alert me to a rivulet suddenly trickling forth from my mind. Now it begins to flow, a clear stream without any obvious source. Death, it seems, has become a mediator between myself and the watery nature of the spirit.

When I look down that road, past a patchwork of shadows, I see clear sunlight and a youth, barely beyond adolescence, dark-haired, with a refined and eager face, gazing towards me, but not *at* me. He seems familiar, I don't know why. And then I begin to recognise, in the fullness of my illness, that this young man is the Other. He stands there with the future ahead of him, ever curious, almost avid, and utterly impervious to the voice of the collective. Already he has made solitude his friend. This is the Other who is about to become myself. *He is me.*

Of course memories intervene. The bush path to the sea, the bottle brush and banksia trees, crabs in their regimented hoards scurrying across mudflats, these are a youth's accumulations, his capital. At that age he is a spendthrift. All the images he acquires are real. They rub against pylons like a rowboat, wearing smooth its gunnel. Childhood is a rich tapestry: the colours of the world are protodelic, the beginning of conscious recognition. When they pass before one's eyes, as one deals with pain in another life, nothing can erase their indelible nature. That youth is like an anemone who absorbs every crepuscular moment, infinity buried in the eternal.

Pain is so immersive that it isolates the sufferer from being. One is forced to live in a kind of leprosarium of the mind. Hope is obliterated. And, as a leper, one is banished to a so-called 'colony' in some remote place, where all human emotion is dismissed by the casual consternation of others, the healthy. Of course pain is the ingenious effort a disease makes in order to survive. Alphonse Daudet, a French writer and fellow sufferer (syphilis), spoke of an attack by 'wasps' followed by the advent of pain, the cruellest of guests. He spoke too of the 'clever way' that death cuts us down, a meadow attacked from several sides by reapers all at the same time.

The Other, in a sense, is one's Angel. I observe its presence as a benign effect. Frequently in my life have I encountered my Other as a positive influence, one governed by *amor fati*, my destiny. Because of it, I have been drawn into experiences that affirm my sense of wonder at the world's primeval order. Things work, I tell myself, and I am merely a small cog in such an altic mechanism.

I am struck by the word, *numen*. In Latin it suggests more than spirit, energy, or the sacred. These words are worn out by overuse. In ancient languages, too, essences often exist in words that go beyond the comfort of the familiar. Cicero identified numen with the divine will. Virgil, also. My task has always been to revive the concept of numen for a modern audience, to alert readers to a state of reverence present in all things.

I have always admired Socrates. He often walked about Athens with bare feet, oblivious to the dismay of those who expected more of him. It seemed he preferred the ground underfoot to the soft compunction of sandals.

***

In the past I have been inspired by a number of men, most of them monks or poets. Basho's journeys to the Deep North of Japan remind me that words and wandering share a unique symbiosis. They feed on one another. Though he was a drunk and sometimes irascible, Basho found a way to extract meaning from his foibles. He made the road into one prolonged Haiku poem, an act of compression that caused prolixity to become outmoded.

At dawn, when I recite the Jesus Prayer, I experience a certain slippage in my being. The prayer circumnavigates my pain, going ashore to nourish and be nourished. As ancient as it is, the prayer nonetheless resonates with all the presumption of freshness. It is like a flower, newly opened to the sun, a ten-petalled bloom of incomparable beauty. Identity and action are perfectly embodied. Because of it, entreaty lands on deck like a god. The words, "Jesus Christ, Son of God, have mercy upon me" (*Kyrie Iisou Christe yie tou Theou eleison me*) make up the amphora into which I dip my cup each day. I can't drink enough of it.

Grasp the light as if it were a nettle. Do not fear it. This is how Dionysius the Areopagite and St Symeon the New Theologian perceived deific light. It is not like the sun or glow of a candle in appearance, not at all. This light emanates from the cosmos, yet remains distant from it. In a sense, *that light is me.* It dances across the surface of my being with all the amplitude of the sun's rays across waves at dusk. But even then it is not visible, not some mysterious photon buried in matter. Deific light (*apistephto phos*) transcends perception because such a light is an irradiation of Spirit, and it stings while it delights.

Each morning I awake to the sound of twittering birds, and the healing power of words. They are synonymous, a kind of pre-lingual banter. Nature and the power of abstraction merge in my mind to form the mortar of a prototypal language. Birds utter words, even if I do not understand them. The turbulent passion of words, Elias Canetti maintained, is to sift one language through another. Thus do I draw upon *mystes* and *logos*, for example, and come up with 'mystery' and 'word'. These are synonymous, too. They awaken me to the twitter of Latin and Greek in their bid to make muteness into wonder. Birds do this in *chorus*. This is precisely what Tuotilo carved into the cover of his *Evangelium longum*. HIC RESIDET XPC VIRTU: 'Herein resides the power and virtue of Christ.' Such a book! His answer, it seems, in response to the healing effects of letters carved in ivory.

Let it be stated: *sono finito*. And again: *j'ai termine*. There, I have sifted my demise through other languages at last. Why not give it a more classical tone: EGO COMPLEVIT: QUIA SUPER HOC? ('I am finished: it is over'). It sounds so perfect, so resolved. This is the nature of departure: to find the right words. No more metaphors, no more heartfelt sentences. Just the smooth transition into finitude. It is the hardest task for anyone to complete because we are in league with hope. And yet, is not hope a coat we should discard, finally, when we glimpse an unearthly sun?

I consent to death. It has made its demands, and I can no longer resist them. I don't know whether it wanted me to fight as much as I have. No matter. Finitude has a way of exercising its claims. My illusion was to have believed that I could dismiss them as unacceptable. Now I see death as a sort of plasma, invisible and yet ever present, fluidly embracing my being. It seeps into my body like water into a dry riverbed after rain, soothing parched earth.

Cioran informs us that the only genuine state of forgetfulness is to sleep in Divinity. Clearly insomniacs are those whose quest has been blocked by their insistence upon recollection.

For me, tears are the residue of Divinity's claim upon me. Their dampness on my cheeks is the unfathomable mystery of the cosmos blending with its Origin.

We have forgotten how to contemplate death *in* ourselves. Obviously it is there, a chrysalis in its cocoon. Our task is to unwind that golden thread and allow it to emerge, in its most precursal form, in order to become a fluttering moth. In that way we realise our own death rather than simply submitting to it.

***

Once, when I was in Mantua, I visited the home of a fifteenth-century noblewoman who retired to her rooms because her father refused to allow her to become a nun. Her asceticism, in a sense, had become suburban. Climbing the stairs to her room, however, I at once felt the power of her ascent. She made me realize how important it is to *climb up to one's own cell.*

Divinity's non-existence fascinates me. It has stepped beyond the validation of words, beyond cosmogenesis itself, to inhabit that region of my thoughts where its image becomes redundant. The futility of wanting to 'approach' Divinity at all: redaction is of its primal essence, not my yearning for it to be.

I am beginning to identify with pain, not because it implies suffering or hurt – but because I realize now that it is as contingent to our body's function as blood. Pain is like an invisible organ, akin to the soul perhaps, that challenges us to celebrate its presence. This is the reason why ascetics are impervious to comfort; they are too intent on cultivating pain as a release from the pleasure of merely being alive.

***

As a boy he found himself apprenticed to his father in Nazareth. Carpentry became his trade, and followed him to Golgotha. Wood: carpentry, cross: martyrdom, something arboreal struck him down in his prime. Not palm or cedar, no – simply that he was an oak of a man whose shade threatened many. In him, selfhood was consumed as wood is by fire, thus reducing it to ashes. Few wished to accept that he was, in fact, the Tree of Life.

Words are beginning to scuttle down hawsers in my mind, rats off a sinking ship. Or is it that they wish to return to their source? Language is a great river streaming forth from the high Alps of the Word itself. A man at a loss for words, as I am becoming, is someone who is reduced to silence. Muteness is the final enclave of the poet. The unutterable is his helpmate.

Some hermits whom I have met demonstrate a capacity to retreat behind their gaze, as if they have undergone a lobotomy. It is not their brain that has been removed, however, nor their memory. But something of their past life has been erased. When I look at them, I realise what 'tunnel-vision' really means. They have lost their sense of seeing anything other than the emptiness of life as a prophylactic. Like gauze, it has been placed over their soul to prevent any illusion of pleasure escaping from their wound. Not that they wish to staunch it. Tears have long since become a provocation for bliss, the final emission of the spirit.

So far, I haven't interrogated my illness, at least not in so many words. Is it because of timidity on my part? Most things, once they are named, enter a state of the familiar. I refuse to allow my condition to become so.

I want to test its durability by leaving it unnamed. Let me assure myself that its very anonymity signals a declension between being and hope. This is the place where survival becomes its own imperative. And yet, it is all a hoax. A battle between antigens and antibodies reminds me that we are always at war within ourselves.

The Latin word SANGUIS teases me with its associations. Derived from the Sanskrit word for 'blood' (*a-srij*), it suggests descent, blood-relation, even spirit. The Greeks and Romans, however, extended it to embrace a broader connotation. Philosophers and emperors adopted young men as their heirs in thought and potential power. Parmenides adopted Zeno as his, Socrates that of Plato, and Emperor Augustus adopted Marcus Aurelius to succeed him. Which leads one to believe that there is an intellectual consanguinity capable of transcending blood-line. Men are drawn into loving association so that they might give a transfusion to one another.

Silence is the sound of the earth emitting noise. It reverberates among mountains and valleys. This sound is made by thought before the birth of language. No wonder hermits rarely talk. They are listening to the desert at the heart of their own ruminations.

It is said of the conch shell that it retains the sound of the sea deep within its maw. Even as an empty form it remains tethered to its origin. I try to imagine whether other natural objects might do the same. I don't hear the echo of the breeze in a dead tree, nor the sound of stone other than when it cracks apart in a fire. Which begs the question: does the conch possess a yearning that even death can't dispel? Will my own body, when it is eventually laid to rest, begin a conversation with the earth?

The entire Christ story is based upon an act of torture (CRUCIO = to torture; FIXUS = a stable object driven into the ground). If this is so, then for some reason Pagan Europe preferred to embrace such a trauma as its own. I ask myself why. Was suffering finally to be given its due? Perhaps men had found in self-sacrifice a more durable purpose. By crucifying themselves, they could invoke the anguish of existence for what it was – none other than a reposte to the endless illusion of pleasure that had yielded little other than Stoicism.

Egyptians were one of the few peoples to transcribe words onto pillars and in tombs. It seems that bare stone was not enough to establish a temple precinct or tomb wall as eternal fixtures. I have never imagined words as architectural adjuncts before, yet 'hieroglyph' does mean 'risen marking'. It is an aid to transcendence. The word rises, as does a pillar or wall. It may be that when words were inscribed onto parchment, they acquired a horizontal character. Once supine, they surrendered their role as intermediaries between men and their gods. It follows that when the Corinthian pillar entered Egypt with the Ptolemys, the gods fell silent.

What is an *escriturist*? A person who makes the act of writing into an extension of his body.

The word 'belief' is an act of conscious thought. Tribal people do not 'believe' because they refuse to act consciously towards their understanding of the Spirit. The Spirit enters them as a formless emanation to be made palpable by the imagination. This is not a conscious endeavor on their part. They are merely serving the Spirit's need to be worshipped.

I've lived many lives in one life. In a sense, I am polynatal. The very word confers a duality of languages upon me. French, Italian, Spanish, Greek, Arabic, Iban, Torajan, Torres Strait Islander and Aboriginal, this great river of humanity has flowed through me. At cafe tables and in bus terminals I have encountered the greatness and suffering of humanity. Not a horseman of the Apocalypse am I, but one whose fleet-footed steed is able to clear obstacles with one leap. Chevalier, jinete, cavaliere, the joy of discovery and flight. Where does the journey end? In prayer, abeisance, in worn hooves and foaming mouth. My saddle is worn, the girth-buckle is tearing at its leather strap. Now I sit under a tree in a Persian miniature and confer with sages. Their voices are the voices of a singular life.

AEVUM - that is, we live in space and time. Already Cicero has anticipated Einstein with his remarks. A curtain is drawn and we witness a stage filled with magical effects that transcend both. These we arrange in keeping with our performance.

It is said that John Scotus Erigena, a prominent medieval theologian, was stabbed to death by his students with their pens because he made them think. An unlikely story, but one that gives us cause to consider. Socrates, too, found himself condemned to death by the sentate for a similar reason. I begin to wonder why thinking should be viewed with such fear and hatred. Does it 'upset the applecart' as they say? Is it because serious thought questions the power of privilege and convention? Pens and words are clearly sharper than swords. Either way, John Scotus and Socrates experienced the pain of this metaphor to their cost.

"A dance of the intellect among words," a timely jig invented by Ezra Pound to denounce the plodding nature of poetry in his time. Where else *can* the intellect be found but among words? Like a rare gem it must be uneartheed, cut and polished. This is the facetous nature of language; it thrives upon playfulness, on cut and thrust. When the intellect begins to dance, then do we engage in an elevation of being, two figures on an ancient drinking cup kicking up their heels.

My body, now, is in violent disagreement with me. It simply refuses to concur with my pre-disposition towards health. It is Mephistophelian in its demeanour – promising much but delivering little. I feel like a termites' nest that has been abandoned, filled with empty passages that once teemed with life. It there were such a thing as a solar eclipse of the body, then I am surrounded by darkness.

The word 'remarkable' holds a strange fascination. It suggests something excellent, notable, a fact to be marveled at. And yet, as 'remark' it alludes to no more than a casual aside. If it is broken down even further, to 're-mark', we are confronted by its true meaning – to make a mark on paper or stone. How can a word settle on its true meaning when faced with such seismic shifts? Unless, of course, it is volcanic by nature.

When I first read Boethius I tried to imagine what it must have been like to confront death in a Pavia cell for treason, and still be able to pen his *Consolation of Philosophy*. In spite of everything, he found the strength to conjure up an angel, Sophia, in order to escape the trauma of the garrot. So this is why men believe in angels. They offer the prospect of ascent and flight when one's thoughts are buried in a mire of anguish.

We never consider the possibility of taking *too much from life*, of overdrawing from vivacity's current account. Instead we regard it as a huge Ponzi scheme that sustains us by drawing upon the level below, filled as it is with gullible participants like ourselves who are eager to emulate what we do. It seems that any sense of balancing the ledger is anathema to those who steal from life.

Two words have a corrosive effect upon open conversation, cynicism and scepticsm. Both are designed to belittle any discussion involving metaphysics or religious belief. In fact, they deny the validity of belief as a concept altogether. It is because cynics and sceptics are beholden to their absolute reliance upon rationalism as a thought process. By definition, neither a cynic nor a sceptic can be a true philosopher because they cannot embrace the uncertainty invested in considered thought as a pathway to revelation.

If I have exceeded my quodidian of life, then it is because avidity has interceded.

If God give us strength to survive, then we suffer gravely when he goes on holidays.

I now know what death smells like. Of decay and deliquescence, the rapid disambiguation of being. It is in my nostils now, a subtle stench that refuses to go away. Philosophers never talk about the smell of death. Like a black tulip it grows in dark earth, a flower whose beauty is blighted by the prospect of decomposition. For philosophers, this is the ultimate reposte to the bright flame of intellect.

The Spirit has no need to be rational. What determines its vitality is that sense of commisseration with the infinite.

A man who denies the existence of Spirit is forever imprisoned in the unenviable contingency of matter.

Spirit may be as ephemeral as smoke, yet it is forever reliant upon that flame which makes it possible.

We know that the atom exists, though it defies all our senses to give it form. Atoms exist because we have formulated a language to capture their reality, namely atomic science. Conversely, we know that Spirit exists in spite of our inability to define it with our senses. Spirit exists because we have devised the language of theology and metaphysics to identify its ethereal form.

Spirit has no properties, other than our inability to define it. As such, Spirit is the only reality immune to the power of words.

To chase after Spirit with words is to feel the wrath of the dragon's tail.

While Spirit escapes all our conceptual apparatus, it nonetheless pervades our being with the full force of air banishing a vacuum. Ibseity, or fullness, is its forte.

I have never known a man imbued with Spirit to be other than someone who accepts eternity as his lodestar.

Lingering too long in life is to reject the value of cessation. An incurable disease is one way to short circuit such a interminable dilemma.

Socrates probably felt that in knowing nothing he knew too much.

Spirit's origin lies in the Greek word *pneuma*, or breath. This accounts for its ever-shifting, invisible nature. Unlike 'soul' which is stable and unmoving, Spirit participates in all, while remaining ever on guard against the possibility of capture. The ultimate escapee, it loves freedom more than constraint. Spirit's motto can only be, of course, *noli mi tangere*, don't touch me.

It's nice to be surrounded by ancient languages, Greek and Latin in particular. They bring to English the warm airs of the Mediterranean, its nimble wit (Greek) and the august rigour of the Latin tongue. Few would argue that these languages do not house all that Western culture has to offer. English is merely their flighty messenger, Hermes, venturing forth from Mt Olympus bearing the logos.

Try not to deal with false emotions for the sake of instant pleasure.

When you retire from the battlefield after a skirmish, remember that the next one may embody your defeat.

The irony of pain is that it does not allow us to experience the fulsome nature of death. Any romance attached to the latter is negated by a body fighting to remain alive.

"One should live as though one's head is on fire," so spoke the Buddha. This presents a real dilemma to many of us, however. How do we douse the flames which then consume us?

POST VERBA

    Finally my little book with no name, my *liber sin nomine*, has been revealed. I imagine it now, and how it has come into being. Like the Nag Hammadi texts unearthed by a farmer in a field by the Nile with his plough, I am in possession of a rare document that I, too, might have discovered in an ancient amphora such as he.

    Like the farmer, I imagine myself taking it home to remove the accumulated debris packed tight in its neck. Inside is a scroll bound by strips of dry leather. As he has done, I accompany him to a dealer in antiquities in Luxor on his next visit to the city. There, after much haggling, he receives a fair price. The dealer in turn arranges for it to be purchased by an antiquarian in the old part of Zurich. It is from this man, bespectacled and learned, that I finally get my hands on this little book of mine.

So much for the workings of the imagination. It helps me to locate what until now has been an elusive document, one that craved a name in lieu of anonymity. But it had to be written first. It had to be unearthed from lost time, brought out into the open at last. The story of a book is as talismanic as any Hand of Fatima or Christian Cross. I am dealing wiht symbols as much as words.

I have always been fascinated with lost documents. They speak of a silent inertia, of words once passionately expressed, yet for some reason or other find themselves hidden away in order to protect them from the forces of aggrievemet that have raged throughout history. The Essene scrolls and the lost books of the Cathars are just two such examples of pilloried works. Their respective truths have been condemned, and so they find themselves lost to time as well as to their unique place in history.

It is the troubled destiny of all lost books, I fear. And it is for this reason that Tuotilo's *Evangelium longum* is so precious. It has come down to us as a rich embroidery from another age when men felt the desire to document their wonder at the written word which embodied truth. Tuotilo's truth was the Word of God, the sacred utterance of a man from Nazareth who chose *not* to write at all. It was left to others to do so for him. Not to write, as Socrates well knew, is a lasting act of rebellion against the fixity of text.

Talismanic, yes. When I first gazed upon the Evangelium in the monastery of St Gall, I realised at once that its effect upon me was as powerful as the Dead Sea scrolls must have been to those archeologists digging inside that cave in Israel. Sacred utterance had been revived; the *Evangelium* lay before me on a table, its jewel-encrusted cover a doorway to a place, an *aevum*, where time and place were molded into one. Together Tuotilo and Sintram had managed to create a garden of words, none other than the Word of God as a fate-filled bed of blooms.

Today this kind of enthusiasm is reserved for scientists in their laboratories. They uncover so-called 'new knowledge', the DNA of memory as Plato attests. But is this knowledge truth, or merely the accumulation of evermore reliable – and contingent – information? While

Einstein's theory of relativity might tantalise with its formulaic exactitude, it is a moot point whether it touches us in the way that an ancient scroll does alongside its carefully crafted words.

Words are the true artifacts of the mind. They are stored among the pages of our neurones like scrolls in a desert library. Sometimes they are lost to us when we fail to acknowledge the truths entrusted to them. In the past, scribes understood the relationship between the act of writing and the thoughts that they provoked. To be a scriptor was thus a sacred discipline. Words contained numen for them, the very stuff of the Spirit.

I have spent a good deal of my life travelling to where men still believe in the value of codified truth. Among the Iban of Borneo, whose bamboo wafers of words are carefully stored in longhouses, to those monasteries in Upper Egypt replete with their musty libraries, to the deserts of Australia where petroglyphs scar rock faces in caves – all this deep knowledge I have wanted to experience for myself. It is, I now know, the knowledge of thought itself emerging from the primeval earth.

Such a passion for language, for words! A coalescence of agreements, a method of unification. Words, after all, unify; they make it possible for disparate impressions to be given a life. It is enough to say that words live in the domain of thought as fish do in the sea. This is their natural environment. Taken out of thought, however, they run the risk of being abased by cliche and dogma. They soon begin to smell as they quickly become tainted.

The aphorism is one way to revive words as a repository of meaning. It deepens it and complexifies the etymology of thought. The aphorism is like a scalpel; it cuts away dead flesh and helps to cleanse the wound of conventional expression. It becomes a mental abrasion that prepares the mind for new understanding, for an extension of consciousness. The link between word and revelation is thus retained just as it is for a tribesman when he incises a petroglyph on a stone slab in a cave, thus invoking the words lying dormant within. He uses his fingers as a scribe does his pen.

Which brings me to the naming of my little book. It has finally emerged from my dialogue with a life wholly lived in the shade of leaves as words. Its aphorisms take me away from prosaic expression into the realm of *elogium* – that is, a shorter, more eliptic form of writing. Writers such as E. M. Cioran and Elias Canetti have revived it in our time, but once again it has fallen into disuse.

Why? Is it because we live in a more prosaic age? In a sense, we are surrounded by words – in newspapers, on TV, and through the internet. There has been an explosion of words in the past fifty years, and the idea of verbal condensation has been lost. It remains to be seen if my little book can keep company with others, Pascal and Paul Valery's among them.

What is the name of my book, then? I liken it to a museum of wonders, once the fashion among scientific minds in sixteenth-century Europe. I wanted my book to house wonders, too, but of another order. The horn of a narwal or a petrified fish are not what I wanted to celebrate. Rather, the strange effervescence of a mind caught between two worlds – that of impending death and the unquenched vitality of an intellect on fire. This is what I wished to capture in my

CODEX MIRACULUM

Yes, a miraclous book, a book that has come out of a condition burnished by doubt. For it is doubt that extracts truth from its shell as an oyster is prized loose from its carboniferous enclave. For me, *Codex miraculum* is a memorium. Like the Gnostic Gospels found in Upper Egypt, it is by its own admittance an heretical text. It blends fiction and fact, insight and intuition, truth and its subversion, and regales us with the prospect of *truth as a lie.* There is no other way to say it. The paradox, the contraditcion, these are ever-present. Only then, I realise, can truth be determined as a re-discovered text, none other than a *Codex miraculum* to rank along side Tuotilo's *Evangelium longum.*

www.ingramcontent.com/pod-product-compliance
Lightning Source LLC
Chambersburg PA
CBHW081339080526
44588CB00017B/2681